LATINO LIFE

MUSIC AND DANCE

by Silvia P. Baeza

Rourke Publications, Inc.

WAUKEGAN PUBLIC LIBRARY, WAUKEGAN, IL

The following sources are acknowledged and thanked for the use of their photographs in this work: Julius Fava pp. 2, 25, 27; The Essential Image/Sheldon Potter p. 8; Claire Rydell pp. 12, 26; James L. Shaffer p. 14; Robert Fried pp. 15, 19; Martin Hutner p. 20; Diane C. Lyell p. 22; Bob Daemmrich p. 30; Richard B. Levine p. 34; AP/Wide World pp. 35, 41, 42; Hazel Hankin/Impact Visuals p. 40; Mark Nohl courtesy NM Magazine p. 44. Map on p. 10 by Moritz Design.

Produced by Salem Press, Inc.

Copyright © 1995, by Rourke Publications, Inc.
All rights in this book are reserved. No part of this work may be used or reproduced in any manner whatsoever or transmitted in any form or by any means, electronic or mechanical, including photocopy, recording, or any information storage and retrieval system, without written permission from the copyright owner except in the case of brief quotations embodied in critical articles and reviews. For information address the publisher, Rourke Publications, Inc., P.O. Box 3328, Vero Beach, Florida 32964.

∞ The paper used in these volumes conforms to the American National Standard for Permanence of Paper for Printed Library Materials, Z39.48-1984.

Library of Congress Cataloging-in-Publication Data
Baeza, Silvia P., 1959-
   Music and dance / by Silvia P. Baeza.
      p.   cm. — (Latino life)
   Summary: Discusses different types of Latino music.
   ISBN 0-86625-545-1
   1. Hispanic Americans—Music—History and criticism—Juvenile literature. 2. Popular music—United States— History and criticism—Juvenile literature. 3. Dance—United States—Juvenile literature. 4. Hispanic Americans—Social life and customs. [1. Hispanic Americans—Music— History and criticism. 2. Popular music—United States—History and criticism.] I. Series.
ML3558.B34 1995
780′.8968073—dc20   95-3718
                                                                     CIP
                                                                  AC MN

First Printing

PRINTED IN THE UNITED STATES OF AMERICA

LATINO LIFE

MUSIC AND DANCE

CONTENTS

Chapter 1	What Is Latino Music and Dance?	6
Chapter 2	Roots	11
Chapter 3	The Southwest: Mexican American Music and Dance	17
Chapter 4	The Northeast: Puerto Rican Music and Dance	29
Chapter 5	The Southeast: Cuban American Music and Dance	33
Chapter 6	Important Latinos in Music and Dance	39
	Glossary	45
	More About Latino Music and Dance	47
	Index	48

Chapter 1

WHAT IS LATINO MUSIC AND DANCE?

Music and dancing are an important part of everyone's life. We all have our favorite songs, and we all like to dance. Sometimes we sing and dance at school. Sometimes we hear music on the radio. We dance at parties. We see people dancing on television and in the movies. Music and dance are everywhere.

One special type of music and dance is Latino music and dance. These are the songs and dances that are special to Latino people. What, exactly, is Latino music and dance? First we need to know what *Latino* means.

A Latino is a Latin American person who has immigrated, or moved, to the United States from a Latin American country. Latinos are people who left their native countries to find a better future in the United States. The native country might be Mexico or Cuba. It might be the U.S. territory of Puerto Rico. Or it might be a country in Central or South America, such as Guatemala or Chile.

Latinos can also be persons of Latin American descent. Many Latinos have lived in the United States all their lives. Their parents or grandparents immigrated to the United States, but these Latinos have been Americans since they were born.

Because Latin Americans have Spanish, Indian, or African roots, the Latinos living in the United States show features of these three races. Most Mexican Americans, or Chicanos, are *mestizos*. That is, they are of mixed Indian and Spanish descent. Many Puerto Ricans have both Indian and African blood in their veins. Many Cuban Americans are black because they are descendants of the African slaves that the Europeans brought to the American continent in the 1500's.

WHERE DO LATINOS LIVE?

Latinos live everywhere in the United States, but very large communities of Latinos live in three main areas:
- The Southwest: southern California, Arizona, New Mexico, and Texas
- The Northeast: New York, New Jersey, Pennsylvania, Massachusetts, Connecticut
- The Southeast: Miami and New Orleans

The Latinos who live in these three areas come mainly from three countries in Latin America. The Latinos living in the Southwest come mainly from Mexico. We call them Mexican Americans or Chicanos. The Latinos living in California are Mexican immigrants, Mexican Americans who moved from New Mexico and Arizona to California, or immigrants from Central American and South American countries, like Guatemala, El Salvador, Colombia, or Chile.

The Latino communities in the Northeast consist of immigrants from many Latin American countries, but in New York half of the Latinos are of Puerto Rican descent.

Finally, the Latinos living in the Southeast, many of them in Miami and New Orleans, are mainly Cuban and Cuban Americans. Many Central and South American immigrants and their children also live in the Southeast.

LATINO MUSIC AND DANCE

Latino music came to the United States with the first Latin American immigrants. They moved to the United States in

Traditional Latina musicians with violins.

search of work and wealth. They brought with them not only their personal belongings but also their traditions: their beliefs, their foods, their clothing, their holidays, their music and dance. All these things go together to make a culture. *Culture* is all the things that make a group of people special or different. Music and dance are a very important part of any culture.

   As soon as they arrived in the United States, the Latin American immigrants tried to create a home that was like their home in the old country. Music and dance played an important role in this process. Latin Americans are a dancing people. They have large family reunions and celebrations with music and dancing. Latinos are also a very religious people. Many Latinos are Catholics, and they often practice their religion through music and dance. In their new home in the United States, Latinos re-created their old culture. They kept their old celebrations and religious festivals, using music and dance. They wanted to remember their past and preserve their special culture.

FOLK MUSIC, POPULAR MUSIC

When we speak of Latino music and dance, we are talking about two types of music: (1) traditional or folk music, and (2) popular music.

The *traditional* or *folk* music and dances came to the United States with the immigrants. Many of the songs and dances that Latinos still sing and dance in the United States are very similar to the old Latin American songs and dances. For example, the *corridos* (ballads) that Latinos sing today in New Mexico are just like the corridos that Mexicans sing.

Popular music is different. You can hear popular music on the radio, on television, and in musical recordings like compact discs, or CDs. Popular Latino music and dances started in the big American cities. Latin musicians took the beat, or *rhythm*, and the songs, or *melodies*, of Latin American music and mixed them with other musical styles, like jazz. The mixture gave birth to popular Latin music. A good example of such a mixture is *salsa*. Salsa is a mixture of American jazz and the rhythms of Puerto Rican or Cuban music. Salsa is very different from the Puerto Rican and Cuban musical forms that gave birth to it.

American bands and recording companies in the United States have done a lot to make Latino music popular. Some bands and some recording companies have changed Latino music. They have made a lot of popular music, but the music is not always as good as the traditional music. As a result, many of us do not understand what Latino music and dance really are. To find out, we must look at the roots of Latin American music and dance. How was it born? How long ago? Who created it? Finally, what happened to it in the United States?

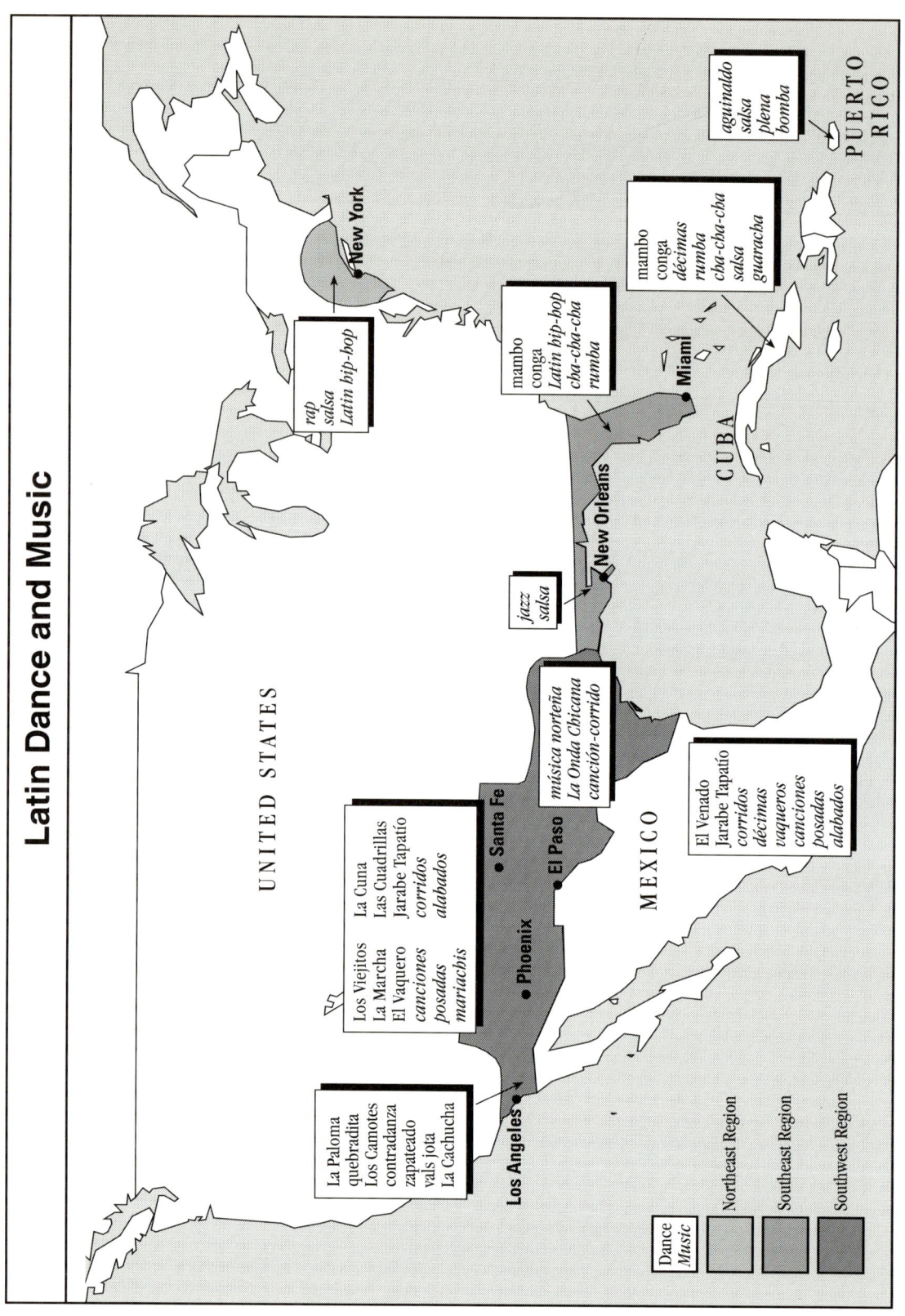

Chapter 2

ROOTS

Latino music and dance were brought to America by the first Latino immigrants who settled in the United States. Most of them came from Mexico, Puerto Rico, and Cuba. Some came from other countries in Central America, South America, and the Caribbean Sea. These immigrants brought songs and dances from their countries. They played and danced them in fiestas and other festivals in America.

To understand the roots of Latino music and dance, we must look at the people who lived in Latin America before Latino immigrants came to the United States. After the Spaniards arrived in America in the fifteenth century, three cultures got mixed in Latin America: the Indian, the Spanish, and the African.

INDIAN ROOTS

The Mayas, Aztecs, and the Incas were the biggest Indian civilizations in Latin America, but there were many other tribes, too. In those times, the Indians did not write down descriptions of their music and dance, but the Spanish explorers who traveled in the Americas did. They wrote descriptions of the Indians' songs and dances in their journals. That is how we know about the Indians' music today.

Music and dance were an important part of the Indians' lives. They believed that people had souls that survived after their death. They held many ceremonies to celebrate the eternal life of their souls. They also believed in many gods and held special events, called rituals, to honor them. For

Some of the Indians' dance rituals were danced by men.

example, at least once every year, they would sing and dance to honor the sun god. They believed that the sun god made the rain and sunshine. The sun god could make the Indians' crops grow, so there would be enough food for the winter. They sang, danced, and played their favorite instruments—especially the flute. The Indians had many different types of flutes, which produced soft melodies. Using music and dance, the Indians thanked their gods for good weather or a good hunt. They prayed for good health and wealth.

All these dances were danced dramas. That is, the dances told a story. The dances lasted many hours, sometimes even days. Some dances could be danced only by the men. Other dances could be danced only by the women. For example, the dances performed during the hunting season were male dances. The men moved around like the animals they were going to hunt. Sometimes the men also made animal sounds.

SPANISH ROOTS

In the sixteenth century, the Spaniards arrived from Europe. They were mostly soldiers, but later other Spaniards came. Some of them were missionaries—men sent to teach the Bible to the Indians. The missionaries taught the Indians to believe in one god and to sing and dance in praise of that God. From the Spaniards, the Indians learned to sing psalms and hymns. The Indians also learned to act in religious plays called *autos sacramentales*. These plays were held in the church. The autos sacramentales told stories about the Eucharist, the bread-and-wine Communion ceremony in honor of Jesus' death.

The Spaniards brought with them many of their traditional instruments. They brought the organ, the violin, the harp, the accordion, the bandoneón, the trumpet, and many different types of guitars. They taught the Indians how to play these instruments and also how to build them. Soon the Indians' music began to change. European violins and guitars sounded different from the Indians' flutes. The rhythms and melodies of the Spaniards' songs were very

Spanish contradanzas were danced in lines of couples, just like some Mexican line dances.

different from the rhythms and melodies the Indians were used to singing.

Together with their music, the Spaniards also brought dances. The most popular dances the Indians learned from the Spaniards were the *danzas, contradanzas, cuadrillas,* and *valses.* These were all court dances danced by the rich people.

When these dances came in contact with the Indians' dances, new types of dances were born. Three kinds of dances grew out of this mixture: religious or ritual dances, dance dramas or festival dances, and folk dances. The Spanish dances had the most influence on the folk dances, like the Jarabe Tapatío of Mexico. In this dance, the dancers lined up in couples. They performed intricate steps and figures like the ones in Spanish dances such as the contradanza. A good example of religious dance is the Devil dance of Bolivia. It was danced at the beginning of Lent, just before Easter. A popular dance drama that is still danced today in Mexico is El Venado, the deer dance. In this dance, the dancers retell a legend about a deer hunt.

AFRICAN ROOTS

In the sixteenth century, another culture arrived in the Americas: people from the continent of Africa. Spaniards and other Europeans made the Africans get on boats, and they took them to America. They made the Africans slaves and sold them as workers. In America, the African slaves had to work long hours on plantations, but during their free time, they gathered to sing and dance.

The rhythms of the Africans' music were new to the Indians and Spaniards. The Africans built their own instruments from memory, because they did not have the

Africans added drums to the mixture that became Latino music.

chance to bring any from Africa. Most of their instruments were *percussive*. That is, the Africans played their instruments by striking them or shaking them. Some of these new percussive instruments were drums, rattles, and bells.

The Africans did not have many flutes, like the Indians. They did not have any violins or guitars, like the Spanish. These instruments already existed in America. Now, with the African drums, music changed even more. New melodies and rhythms were created. New songs and dances were born.

Not all new music and dance showed the same amount of African and Indian influence. In some regions of Latin America, African music mixed only with Spanish music. In Cuba, for example, the Indians were killed by the Spaniards or they died from diseases that the Spaniards brought with them. Since no Indian music survived, the African music mixed with the Spanish music to make Afro-Cuban rhythms and dances. Afro-Cuban music and dance are very different from Indian music and dance. In Cuba, the dances are a lot like African dances. Some of the Latin American dances that started as African dances are the *conga and rumba* of Cuba, the *samba* and *batuque* of Brazil, and the *cumbia* and *porro* of Colombia.

Contemporary Roots

In Latin America, music has always had two purposes: entertainment and communication. Music for entertainment is played at fiestas and in nightclubs. Music for entertainment is often about love and friendship.

Music for communication can also be played at fiestas, but usually it is played at concerts. Music for communication tells about the social and political problems that people face every day. These songs ask questions: Who are Latin Americans? Are they free? Are they not free? How do people live? In wealth or in poverty? Many musicians have written songs that try to answer these questions. Music for communication is a very important part of Latin American music. It became very important for Latino music in the United States, too.

Chapter 3

THE SOUTHWEST: MEXICAN AMERICAN MUSIC AND DANCE

People of Spanish and Indian blood have lived in the Southwest and Mexico since the sixteenth century. The city of El Paso, Texas, was started by Spaniards in 1598. Spaniards founded the city of Santa Fe, New Mexico, in 1609. By 1760, New Mexico had thousands of Spanish settlers, and there were more than two thousand Spanish settlers in Texas.

There were not many Anglo-American settlers in the Southwest until the 1820's, after Mexico became an independent country. Then, in 1846, the United States fought a war with Mexico. The United States took a lot of land that belonged to Mexico, and later it bought more territory from Mexico. This land became part of the United States: California, Arizona, New Mexico, and Texas.

Many Mexicans already lived on the land that the United States now owned. Even though the United States now owned this land, the Mexican people who lived there still spoke Spanish. They still thought their culture was Mexican. Since then, many more Mexicans have crossed the Mexican border and have settled in the Southwest. For many Mexicans and Mexican Americans, the Southwest has been their home for hundreds of years.

Traditions in the Southwest

In the Southwest, music and dance play an important role in everyday life. The social life of Mexican Americans has always centered on family, religion, and history: religious holidays, birthday parties, christenings, and weddings. Music and dance are the most popular entertainment during these occasions.

Since the Mexican territories became part of the United States, Mexican Americans have tried to preserve their traditional music and dance. Today, for example, traditional street bands called *mariachis* still play at festivals and on holidays. They sing traditional songs: *décimas*, *canciones*, *posadas*, *alabados*, *vaqueros*, and *corridos*. The décima is a ballad. The canción is a sentimental song, often about love. Posadas are Christmas songs. Alabados are religious songs of praise. Vaqueros are cowboy songs. Corridos are ballads that tell about the adventures of ordinary people.

California

Alta California is the old name for the American state of California. The first Spaniards and Mexicans settled in Alta California in 1769. For many years, the Spanish missionaries built missions in California. Each mission was like a small town. At the center was a Catholic church, where the missionaries taught the Indians the Catholic religion. After the missions, the Spaniards built presidios (fortresses) to protect the missions. Then they built quiet little pueblos (towns). First came San Diego in 1769, then Monterey in 1770, then San Francisco in 1776, and finally Santa Barbara and Los Angeles in 1781.

In the Southwest, mariachi bands play traditional Mexican music at festivals and on holidays.

The rich people got together at *bailes* (balls). These bailes were fancy dance parties for the upper class. California's most popular dance was the *contradanza*, a court dance that the Spaniards had first brought to Mexico. In the contradanza, two lines of dancers face each other and dance in complicated figures and steps. There were many types of contradanzas in different areas of California. Some were danced in circles; others were danced in straight lines. Another popular group dance in California was the *vals jota*, a type of waltz. The vals jota was a lively, fast-moving dance, and it was especially popular among the people in Santa Barbara and Los Angeles.

Not all California settlers were from the upper class. Many lower-class Mexicans left Mexico for Alta California and started *ranchos* (ranches) to raise cattle and *haciendas* (plantations) to grow grain and vegetables. They became *rancheros* (ranchers). The music and dances at the ranchos and haciendas were very popular.

The rancheros did not have bailes. Instead, they had *fandangos*. Fandangos were dancing parties for the working people. At the fandangos, the people danced folk dances instead of the contradanza or the vals jota. The most popular folk dances of California were Los Camotes, La Paloma, and La Cachucha. These dances are still danced today in California. Other folk dances that existed then have disappeared. La Sarna, El Cuando, and El Pontorico were lost. Today nobody can dance them; the music and steps have been forgotten.

Bailes and fandangos were not the only parties the Mexican Americans had in California. Other celebrations included fiestas, or festivals. Mexican American festivals were like carnivals, with parades, beautiful horses, and riders who sat on decorated saddles. Women dressed in old California dresses. Bands played old California music, and couples dance old California dances. One of these carnivals took place the week before Lent. It was called *baile de*

Today, banda music is a favorite of young Latinos, especially in Los Angeles.

cascarones. It was a colorful festival filled with bright costumes, loud music, and merry dances.

Today California has become the cradle for another music and dance style: *banda*. Banda music started more than a hundred years ago, in the small towns of Mexico. Mexican *orquestas* (orchestras, or groups of people who played music together) used to play in the public plazas of these small towns. Their main instruments were violins, drums, trumpets, and tubas. Today, banda musicians have added accordions, electric bass guitars, horns, and synthesizers. The result is a Mexican folk music with a carnival flavor.

The banda music has a strong beat and is very exciting. It makes people want to dance. The steps are like the steps in two traditional dances, the *zapateado* and the *quebradita*. The zapateado uses strong foot stamping, called clogging. (Another dance that uses clogging is the flamenco dance, from Spain.) The quebradita is a dance that combines four other dances: two-step, salsa, flamenco, and tango. A movement from the quebradita that the banda dance uses is the back bend. The male dancer arches his partner backward and rocks her gently from side to side.

Today, young people, especially in Los Angeles, like to dance to banda music. Some young people like banda even more than rap and rock. It may be only a craze, but banda is very popular. For Latino youth, banda shows the importance of Mexican Americans in the California community.

NEW MEXICO AND ARIZONA

Two types of dances existed in northern Mexico before the United States got the land from Mexico: folkloric dances and social dances. Folk dances were made popular by the common people in fiestas. The social dances came from Europe to Mexico and were made popular by the upper-class people in bailes. Mexican Americans continued to perform these two types of dances after the United States

bought Arizona and New Mexico, and they still do. Some folk dances still danced in New Mexico and Arizona are La Marcha, Las Cuadrillas, El Vaquero, and La Cuna.

Mexican Americans have also kept their music and dance by performing plays with music. The Spaniards brought religious plays, like the autos sacramentales, to Mexico in the sixteenth century. These plays were shown in the public square or in courtyards. Non-religious plays, like the *representaciones*, or pastoral dialogues, came later, in the seventeenth century. They told stories, with dialogue, songs, and dances.

Traditional music and dance are part of most folk festivals in New Mexico and Arizona. Most of these folk festivals are religious festivals, like El Día de los Muertos (the Day of the Dead) and La Fiesta de Nuestra Señora de Guadalupe (the Feast of Our Lady of Guadalupe). El Día de los Muertos is celebrated on November 2 to remember loved ones who have died. Families get together to decorate the graves of their relatives with flowers and candles. After decorating the graves, the families have a feast with lots of food, music, and dance. La Fiesta de Nuestra Señora de Guadalupe is celebrated on December 12 in honor of the patron saint of Mexico.

Finally, La Navidad, Christmas, is celebrated with Las Posadas, one of the most popular Mexican American festivals. Las Posadas is a nine-day celebration of Mary and Joseph's search for shelter in Bethlehem. It begins with people praying and reading Bible passages about the Nativity. After praying, the people march through the streets holding candles. A boy and a girl, dressed as Mary and Joseph, lead the candlelight procession. People pray the rosary and sing Advent songs as they walk to a nearby house. At the house, they sing verses to ask the people who live there for shelter (*posada*). The house is like the inn where Mary and Joseph asked for shelter. Everybody is invited into the house, and Mexican foods like tamales are served. The children break a *piñata*, an animal-shaped

A blindfolded boy tries to break the piñata with a stick during Las Posadas.

figure filled with candies and nuts, and feast on the goodies that fall to the ground.

Las Posadas is a very symbolic celebration. Everything that happens in this festival has a meaning. The candlelight procession is a symbol of each person's search for God. The invitation into the home is a symbol of the people's acceptance of God into their hearts. Breaking the piñata symbolizes people's rejection of evil. The candy that falls from the piñata is a symbol of God's grace.

Not all festivals are purely religious. The Fiesta de Santa Fe (Santa Fe Festival) celebrates the conquest of the city of Santa Fe by Spain. (The Spaniards reconquered it in 1692 after the Pueblo Indians had occupied it in 1680.) It is held in the capital of New Mexico, Santa Fe, and it lasts several days. People dress in old costumes, sing old corridos, act in old plays, and perform old dances.

Cinco de Mayo (Fifth of May) celebrates the victory of the Mexican Army over the French Army in 1862. Today, this holiday is more important in the United States than it is in Mexico. Latinos in the United States attend festivals where there is much music and dancing. In the schools, children prepare dance programs for their parents. They dance folk dances such as the Jarabe Tapatío and Los Viejitos.

TEXAS

In the 1920's, two musical forms, the *canción* (sentimental song) and the *corrido* (ballad-story), overlapped. Together they formed the *canción-corrido*. Many people still called this new type of song *corrido*.

The corrido was very important all over the Southwest, especially in Texas. Latino singers and songwriters called troubadours began to use the corrido to tell stories about life in the Southwest. These songs were about what it was like to live near the border between Mexico and the United States. The words told about the problems between Anglos and Mexicans, the hard life of the immigrant picking fruit

Cinco de Mayo is a day for festivals, dancing, and music. It honors the victory of Mexico over France in 1862.

One important type of Latino music near the Texas-Mexico border is conjunto. In conjunto bands, the accordion is an important instrument.

or washing dishes, and run-ins with the immigration authorities. These songs were often sad and sometimes funny. They became very popular during the 1920's, 1930's, and 1940's. A well-known corrido was "El Corrido de Gregorio Cortez," about a famous folk hero. The story told by this corrido became a movie in 1982. Corridos are still popular, and they still tell about the lives of Mexican Americans. Today, corridos often sing about discrimination against Mexican Americans.

Texas is also known for a type of music called *música norteña*. Música norteña is another important part of the musical tradition of the U.S.-Mexican border. There are two types of música norteña: *conjunto* music and *orquesta tejana* (Texan orchestra music).

Conjunto music started with the accordion, the *bajo sexto* (a twelve-string guitar), and the *tambora de rancho* (the ranch drum). These instruments made a band that would play at festivals in south Texas. The band would play dance tunes, including the *huapango*, a native dance from the Gulf

Coast of northern Mexico. The accordion became the most important instrument in the band, and the dance beat sounded a lot like the German polka. That was no surprise: Germans had settled in the same area during the nineteenth century. By the 1930's, conjunto music was so popular that music companies were making recordings to sell all over the United States. Even though conjunto is played all over America, many Mexican Texans still think of it as their own special music.

The other type of música norteña is orquesta tejana, or just orquesta, a type of Mexican orchestra. The orquesta began to appear in the 1920's. It was different from the conjunto bands: The orquesta always had a violin or two, usually a guitar, and sometimes other instruments. The players were often from the working class, and sometimes they wore Mexican folk or cowboy costumes. They would play traditional Mexican music at weddings, birthdays, and patriotic festivals like Cinco de Mayo or Dieciséis de

The orquesta is a big band that plays many different kinds of traditional Mexican dance music, as well as some modern music.

Septiembre (Mexican Independence Day). These orquestas sounded a lot like mariachi bands.

In the 1930's, orquestas turned into dance bands. These orquestas were bigger and had more instruments, including trumpets, trombones, and saxophones. Now they played swing and ballroom dance music, as well as traditional Mexican music. Other orquestas still played the old ranchero polkas. The most important orquestas came from Texas and spread across the United States. Music companies sold many recordings of orquesta music played by groups such as Little Joe y La Familia. In the 1970's, Little Joe created a new sound by combining the orquesta sound with rock and jazz. The new music was called La Onda Chicana (Chicano Wave).

Orquesta music combined many American and Latino styles: traditional, jazz, big-band, rock. It was very popular all over the United States from the 1940's through the 1970's. During these years, many Latinos worked to become part of the mainstream American scene. In the 1980's, orquesta lost this broad popularity, but it is still popular in Texas.

Chapter 4

THE NORTHEAST: PUERTO RICAN MUSIC AND DANCE

For Puerto Ricans, music and dance are more than a form of entertainment. If we look at the lives of Puerto Ricans in New York City, we will understand why. For many people, New York is a city of opportunities. New York offers jobs, a mixture of cultures, and all the art forms, including music and dance. However, not all people who live in New York have the same opportunities to enjoy its advantages.

Many Puerto Ricans are very poor. They come from large families and often they cannot get a good education. Some drop out of school to get a job, but they find no good jobs without a high school diploma. Even those who finish high school find it hard to get ahead. Many Puerto Ricans in New York become dishwashers, street cleaners, and doormen. Money is scarce and hopes are low for these New York Puerto Ricans, or *Nuyoricans*.

Puerto Ricans are people who love music, and they give it a special place in their everyday life. After working hard in jobs that give them little satisfaction, they often spend their weekends enjoying the only entertainment they can

Puerto Rican children playing traditional Puerto Rican instruments.

afford: dancing. A night at the dance club helps them forget their hard lives. Music and dance also give Puerto Ricans a way of remembering their identity—who they are. Their music and dance allow them to say, "I am somebody. I am Puerto Rican."

Many Puerto Ricans can play a musical instrument. Often, Puerto Rican musicians play on the streets for the people passing by. People stop to listen and sometimes dance. Bands play their music wherever they can, at weddings and at private parties. For example, friends might get together to build a *casita*, a Puerto Rican wooden house. As they build the house, they will play music and sing. Listening and singing makes the work easier. The sad times are merrier.

Salsa Music

What kind of music do Puerto Ricans like? The most popular style is called "salsa." The word *salsa* means "sauce" or "spice." Salsa is a Latin flavor, not only in food but also in music and dance. Salsa has become an important form of music for all Americans of Afro-Caribbean descent: Puerto Ricans, Cuban Americans, and Dominican Americans. Today, salsa is very popular among all Latinos and other Americans, too.

Salsa was born in the 1960's, but not everything about salsa is new. Salsa songs are based on traditional Cuban rhythms like the *rumba, guaracha, mambo,* and *cha-cha-cha.* Puerto Rican musicians borrowed from the Cuban *son* and the *clave* to create this new style. The son is a type of song using African rhythms and African instruments: the *maracas, claves*, and *bongos.* The clave is a type of beat, like a thread that brings together all the different rhythms played by the percussive instruments.

Other characteristics of salsa music make it very different from the old Cuban rhythms. The old mambo, for example, has a set rhythm and beat that cannot be changed. The rhythms and beats of salsa are not set. Thanks to the clave, salsa has a very free style. It is almost like a new musical language with timeless and endless beats and rhythms. The musicians can *improvise* when they play salsa. When they improvise, they are creating the music as they play it—they make up the music as they go along.

Salsa also took elements from Puerto Rican songs like the *bomba,* the *plena,* and the *aguinaldo.* The bomba is a type of song that plantation workers sang and danced. Each bomba has verses of four lines. The verses are sung to the sound of a drum, also called a bomba. In the bomba, the dancers lead the drummers—not the other way around, as it usually is. The plena is a local story set to music, usually sung by townspeople. It is lively, with funny words, and it is accompanied by many different percussive instruments. The aguinaldo is a religious song played during the Christmas season with special musical instruments: gourds, scrapers, maracas, the cuatro, güiros, and the guitar. The music of the bomba, plena, and aguinaldo came together in

Nuyorican salsa. Different musical instruments also came together: the maracas, the güiro, and the cuatro.

Salsa music has words, too. The words of the songs are very important. Old Puerto Rican songs usually did not have a message, but salsa was born because Puerto Ricans wanted to say something. Salsa songs tell stories about the roots of Puerto Ricans and about the kind of life they live in the United States. The songs tell stories about love, friendship, and the problems of living.

Rubén Blades is a leading salsa singer. Many of his songs paint a picture of Puerto Ricans' lives. In some of his songs, Blades sings about Latin Americans who have lost their freedom. Two of his most famous songs are "El Número 6" ("Waiting for Number 6") and "Pablo Pueblo." "El Número 6" tells the story of a Puerto Rican man waiting for the Number 6 train at the subway station. The train is always late, and the man must wait for it every day. "Pablo Pueblo" tells about a man who returns home after work. He returns to his barrio (neighborhood), to the same poor corner, under the same street lamp, to the same street full of trash.

BLACK-PUERTO RICAN RAP

In the 1960's, Puerto Rican and black musicians living in New York formed musical bands. In the beginning, they played black rock-and-roll with Afro-Cuban rhythms. Then came rap music.

When rap music first appeared in the 1970's, young Puerto Rican boys were drawn to it. The Puerto Rican kids had grown up watching and listening to African American youth rapping in the streets and in the school hallways. Now black and Puerto Rican kids were singing together. This mixture was soon accepted in the Puerto Rican barrios.

Today Puerto Rican rap musicians rap in Spanish. Rick Rodriguez and Tony Boston are two Nuyoricans who rap in "Spanglish," a mixture of Spanish and English. There is also a bilingual rap group called Latin Empire. Its singers are Puerto Ricans who were born and raised in New York.

Chapter 5

THE SOUTHEAST: CUBAN AMERICAN MUSIC AND DANCE

In 1959, a great revolution took place in the island country of Cuba. For years, the government had helped a few rich Cubans but had ignored most of the people. The people were poor. They worked very hard, but most of their labor made the rich people richer. The people felt so unhappy that many of them were willing to fight a war against the government. They fought a revolution and won.

After the revolution, the new leader, Fidel Castro, began a Communist government. This new government took the rich people's wealth and kept it in the people's name. The richer Cubans were forced to flee Cuba. They went to the United States, to Florida, only ninety miles across the water. There, the Cubans got help from the United States government.

MIAMI, FLORIDA

Unlike the Puerto Rican immigrants, who were mainly poor people, the early Cuban immigrants were rich people. In Cuba, they had been doctors, lawyers, bankers, and

Traditional Cuban dancers perform in New York City.

owners of businesses. They settled in Miami. They spoke Spanish, and soon the city began to change the names of streets and businesses from English to Spanish. With time, the Cuban immigrants did many good things for Miami and the United States. They started businesses. They created jobs. Miami and its economy prospered.

Cubans brought their most popular music and dance to Miami. Suddenly the rhythms of the son and the guajira began to be danced. Americans had heard these songs before, when traveling singers brought them to New York in the 1930's and the 1940's. Then they were something unusual—new and rare. In the 1950's, right before the Revolution, Cuban music became popular in the United States in nightclubs and through television shows like *I Love Lucy*. In that television show, the Cuban musician Desi Arnaz played Lucy's husband, Ricky. He owned a nightclub where he played conga drums and sang both popular and folk tunes from his native country, Cuba.

I Love Lucy did not showcase all, or even the best, Cuban music, but it made many Americans become interested in Cuban music and dance. Some of the most popular dances were the conga, rumba, mambo, and cha-cha-cha. All these dances used *syncopation*, accented beats that break the regular pattern of the music. The conga was danced in couples or in a line, and the syncopation was expressed with a kick or a flick of the foot. The rumba was also

Desi Arnaz appeared with Lucille Ball in the 1950's television show I Love Lucy. *As Ricky Ricardo, the owner of a nightclub called the Tropicana, he sang Cuban songs and played conga drums, introducing many Americans to Cuban music for the first time.*

danced in couples. With flexed knees, the dancers moved two quick steps and one slow step. The rumba gave rise to the mambo and the cha-cha-cha, which had slightly different steps, but always the same syncopated beat.

NEW ORLEANS, LOUISIANA

Not all Cubans settled in Florida. Some Cuban immigrants went to other places in the United States. Many Afro-Cubans had lived in New Orleans since the end of slavery, so that city was a comfortable place for Cubans.

New Orleans has always been a cradle for new musical traditions. In New Orleans, music has always been played at social occasions, but in the nineteenth century a new type of music was born: *jazz*. Jazz developed as a mixture of African and European music. For example, some Irish and Scottish folk melodies were played with off-beat accents. When jazz was born, New Orleans did a lot to help develop this new type of music. Many musicians were born in New Orleans or moved there, and they helped create the vocal (singing) patterns and the special ways of playing musical instruments that came to be known as jazz. The earliest jazz improvisation was called "New Orleans jazz."

Of all the Cuban immigrants who settled in New Orleans, the Afro-Cubans were most important in the development of jazz. In New Orleans, African American music and Afro-Cuban music came together. There, African American and Afro-Cuban musicians worked together, mixing American and Cuban rhythms. Two of these musicians were Dizzy Gillespie, an African American, and Chano Pozo, an Afro-Cuban. Some of their most famous songs were "Manteca," "Cubana Be, Cubana Bop," "Tin Tin Deo," and "Afro-Cuban Suite." They used the son and clave beat as the base for their music.

It was not until Afro-Cuban music came to America that African American music began to show the simultaneous rhythms and multiple rhythmic patterns that are typical of African music. Thanks to the Afro-Cuban musicians who

Dances from Latin America

Dance Name	Country	Type of Dance
Bamba	Mexico	Social dance
Bambuco	Colombia	Social dance
Bomba	Puerto Rico	Social dance
Banda	Mexico	Social dance
Cha-cha-cha	Cuba	Ballroom dance
Conga	Cuba	Social dance
Corrido	Mexico	Social dance
Cumbia	Colombia, Panama	Social dance
El Venado	Mexico	Social dance
Guajira	Cuba	Social dance
Habanera	Cuba	Ballroom dance
Jarabe Tapatío	Mexico	Traditional dance
Joropo	Venezuela	Social dance
Los Viejitos	Mexico	Traditional dance
Mambo	Cuba	Ballroom dance
Matachines	Mexico	Ceremonial dance
Merengue	Dominican Republic, Venezuela	Social dance
Plena	Puerto Rico	Social dance
Rumba	Cuba	Ballroom dance
Salsa	Cuba, Puerto Rico	Social dance
Samba	Brazil	Social dance
Seis	Puerto Rico	Social dance
Tango	Argentina	Social dance

brought African rhythms into the United States, African American music is what it is today.

Salsa music, which is discussed in Chapter 4, is as important to Cuban Americans as it is to Puerto Ricans. It is also the most "American" of Cuban American music, because it combines the sounds of American jazz with the son and clave of Afro-Caribbean music. Today many Latinos—whether Mexican American, Puerto Rican, or

Cuban American—think of salsa as "their" music. Americans of other backgrounds enjoy salsa, too.

THE SECOND WAVE OF CUBAN IMMIGRATION

In 1980, a second wave of Cuban immigration took place. It started with the "Mariel boat lift," because the Cubans came to the United States in small boats from the small Cuban town of Mariel. This time they were not rich land owners and businessmen. This time they were poor black immigrants. About 125,000 Cubans immigrated to the United States during the Mariel boat lift.

After the Mariel boat lift, even more Cuban rhythms flooded the air. Musicians began to use them in popular American music. The most popular of the new Cuban American music was "Latin hip-hop," or "free style." It swept the East Coast during the 1980's. Latin hip-hop was a style created by young people in New York for young people. It found many fans—not only in New York but also in Florida among Cubans and Cuban Americans who enjoyed visiting Miami's dance clubs.

Chapter 6

IMPORTANT LATINOS IN MUSIC AND DANCE

It is clear that Mexican Americans, Puerto Ricans, and Afro-Cubans have brought great changes to the music and dances of the United States. If Americans dance with excitement to the sound of a corrido in New Mexico or California, it is thanks to the Mexicans and Mexican Americans who have kept this tradition alive. If New York's streets are filled with salsa sounds and both Latino and Anglo Americans dance to salsa, we owe it to the Puerto Rican and Cuban immigrants. If American musicians use African rhythms in combination with American jazz, it is because Afro-Cubans shared their music with them. Many Latinos have contributed to the world of music and dance; here are just a few of them.

Ray Barretto (born 1929): Band leader. He was born in New York of Puerto Rican parents. He was the Musician of the Year and the Best Conga Player of the Year in 1977 and 1980.

Rubén Blades, the Panamanian-born salsa singer, writes and sings songs about the hard life of Puerto Ricans in the city.

Rubén Blades (born 1948): A singer from Panama. He writes salsa songs that tell about the social and political problems of Latinos. Two of his best songs are "Pablo Pueblo" and "El Número 6."

Celia Cruz (born between 1925 and 1930?): A salsa singer and dancer from Havana, Cuba. She came to the United States in 1957 and became a U.S. resident in 1961. She made many albums with Tito Puente, and she is known as the "Queen of Salsa."

Gloria Estefan made traditional Cuban dance rhythms, like the conga, popular with many young Americans in the 1980's.

Gloria Estefan (born 1957): A Cuban American singer and dancer. She became famous with her hit "Conga" in 1989. In 1990, she was hurt in a terrible accident, and the doctors did not think she would walk again. She exercised and worked hard, and today she can walk *and* dance. She has made records and CDs in both Spanish and English.

Freddy Fender (born 1937): A Mexican American from San Benito, Texas. He came from a family of farmers and became a famous U.S. pop singer. His song "Before the Next Teardrop Falls" was a hit in 1975.

Sergio Mendes (born 1941): A Brazilian pianist and composer. His music is a mixture of piano jazz and Latin American rhythms. He toured the United States, where he finally settled.

Rita Moreno (born 1931): A Puerto Rican actor and dancer. Moreno was one of the first Latinas to gain fame on Broadway. One of her most famous roles was as the sister of María in the movie *West Side Story* (1961). She was listed in the *Guinness Book of World Records* as the only performer to win all of the top four awards for performing arts: an Academy Award, a Grammy, a Tony, and two Emmys.

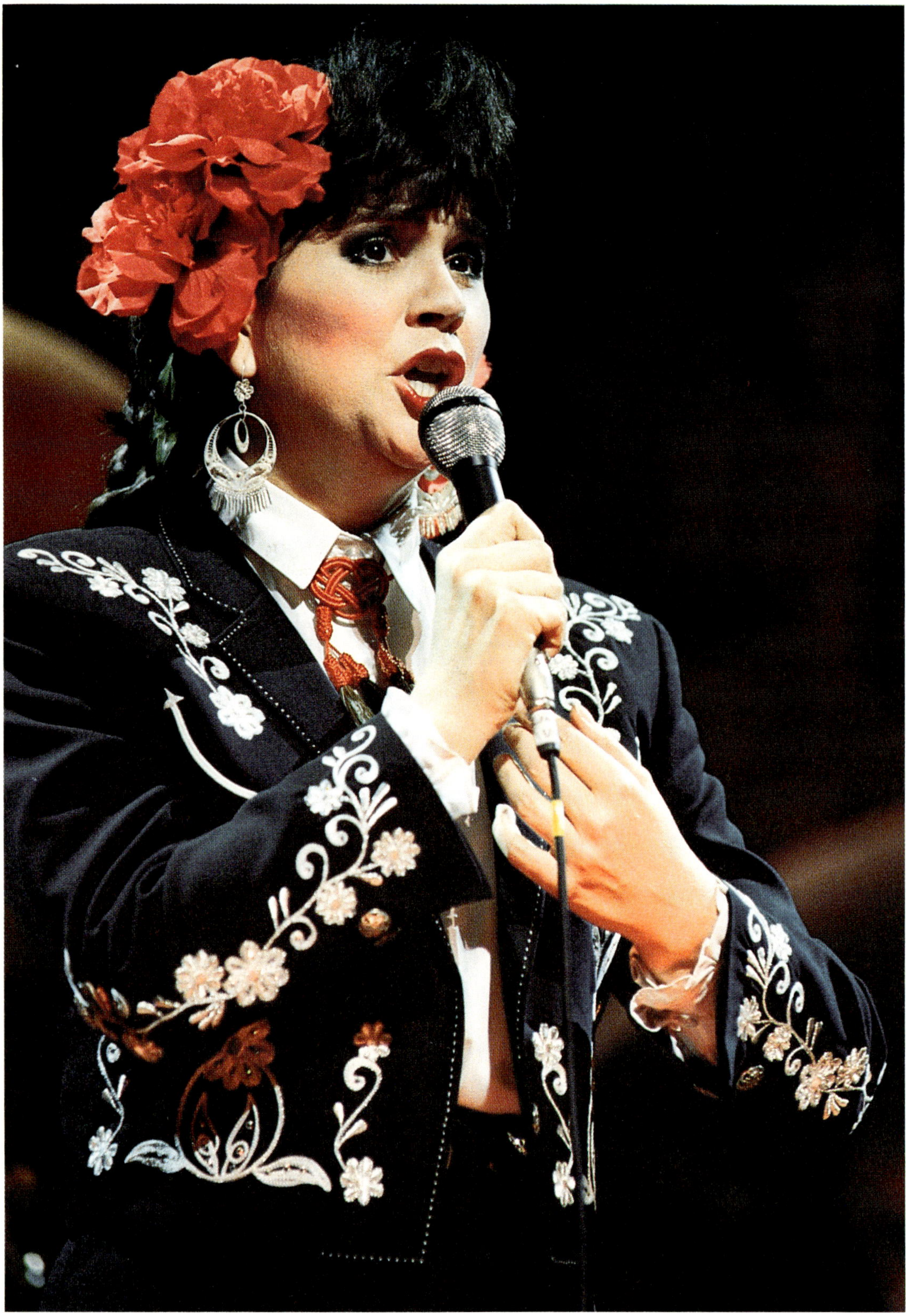

Linda Ronstadt is known both for her popular music and for singing traditional Mexican American folk songs.

Tito Puente (born 1923): A drummer born in New York of Puerto Rican parents. He is known for his many mambo and cha-cha-cha albums.

Chita Rivera (born 1933): Actor and dancer. Rivera rose to fame in dancing Broadway shows in the 1950's (including *West Side Story* in 1957 and *Bye Bye Birdie* in 1961) before going on to a brilliant career in film as well as theater. She starred in the movie *Sweet Charity* (1969). She has won the Tony Award and was inducted into the Television Hall of Fame in 1985.

Linda Ronstadt (born 1946): A singer from Tucson, Arizona. She first sang with her sisters in The Three Ronstadts. She sings many styles of music: country/rock, country, rock-and-roll, opera, and Mexican American folk songs such as corridos.

Carlos Santana (born 1947): The leader of an Afro-Latin rock band called Santana. He is a Mexican American from California and started his band in San Francisco in the 1960's. He used Mexican and Afro-Cuban rhythms and instruments to compose such hits as "Samba Pa Ti."

Ritchie Valens (1941-1959): The first Latino musician who brought together rock and Latino music. He mixed the beat of Mexican and Chicano songs with rock-and-roll rhythms. One of his most popular songs is "La Bamba."

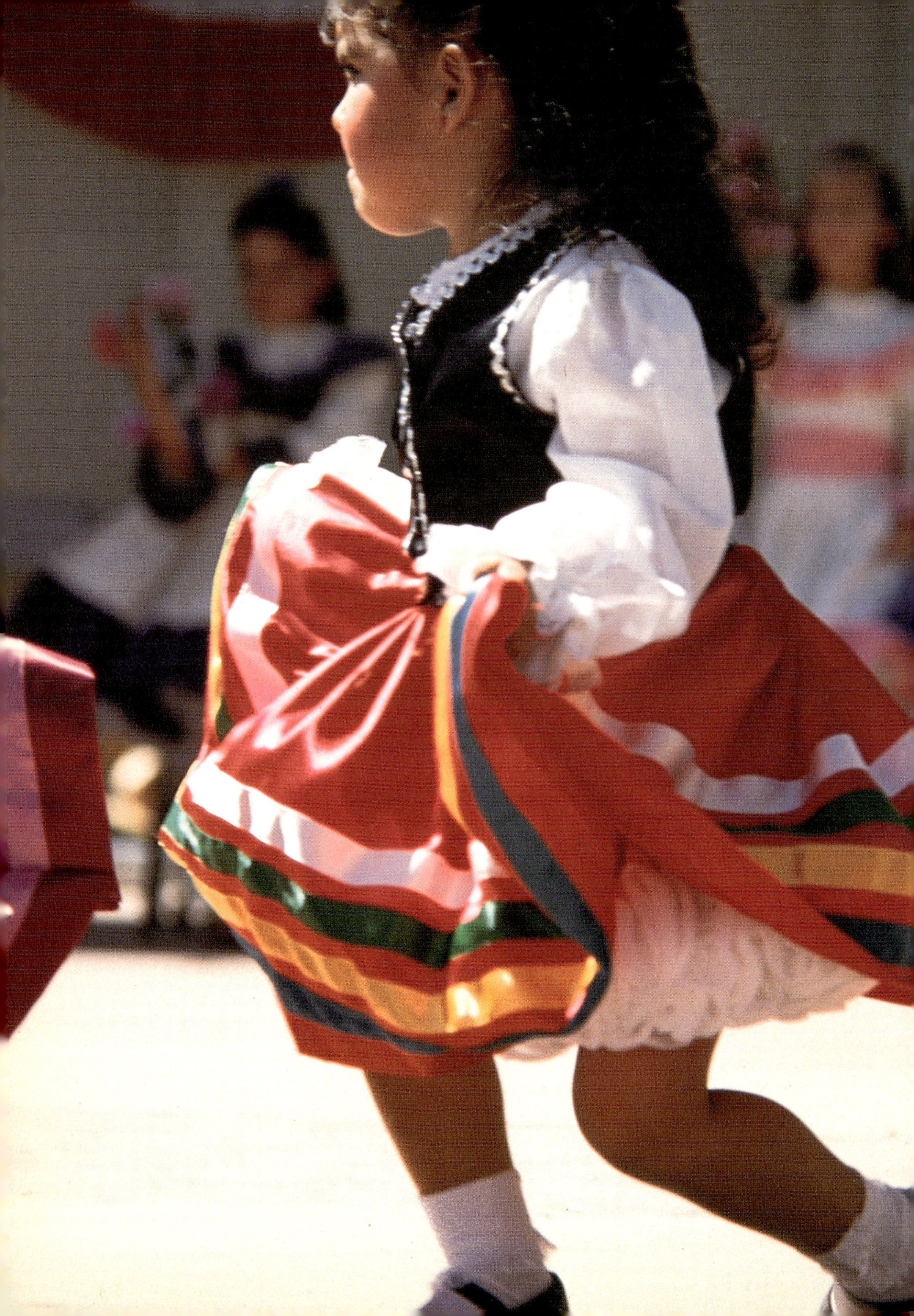

GLOSSARY

accordion: A musical instrument that is played by pumping air into it with one hand and fingering a keyboard with the other hand.

aguinaldo (ah-gwee-NAHL-doh): A religious song played during Christmas.

alabado (al-ah-BAH-doh): A religious song of praise.

baile (BAH-lay): A ball or fancy dance party.

bajo sexto (BAH-hoh SEX-toh): A twelve-string guitar.

banda (BAN-dah): A type of dance, based on traditional Mexican orquesta music, that is very popular with young people, especially in Los Angeles.

bandoneón (bahn-doh-nee-OHN): A type of accordion used in Argentina, Uruguay, and Brazil as a solo instrument or in a band to accompany a tango dance.

batuque (bah-TOO-kay): A Brazilian dance.

bomba (BOM-bah): A Puerto Rican music and dance that has African rhythms.

bongos: A pair of drums from Cuba that are played with bare hands while holding the drums between the knees.

campanitas (cam-pahn-NEE-tas): Bells made of metal, single or in pairs.

canción (can-see-OHN): A sentimental song.

cascabel (cas-cah-BEL): A rattle made of dried seeds, terra-cotta, carved wood, or metal.

castanets: Two wooden shell-shaped clappers made of chestnut wood (*castaña*) and held together by a string.

cencerro (sen-SAY-rroh): A cowbell used as a percussive instrument.

cha-cha-cha: A Cuban social dance that came from the mambo.

charango (cha-RAN-goh): A small lute-shaped instrument like a guitar.

clave (CLAH-vay): The rhythm or beat typical of Afro-Cuban music. *Claves* are instruments used to make this beat.

conga: A type of Afro-Cuban drum that is tall and shaped like a barrel. Also a type of dance.

conjunto (cohn-HOON-toh): A type of Mexican American folk music played by a band with accordion, guitars, and drums.

contradanza (con-trah-DAN-zah): A European court dance brought to the Caribbean by the Spaniards.

corrido (coh-RREE-doh): A ballad that tells a story about the adventures of ordinary people.

cuadrilla (kwah-DREE-yah): A court dance danced by rich people.

cuatro (CUAH-tro): A small, four-string guitar.

cucharas (koo-CHAH-ras): Spoons made of wood or metal and used as percussive instruments.

cumbia (COOM-bee-ah): A Colombian dance.

danza (DAHN-zah): Dance.

décima (DAY-see-mah): A ballad.

fandango (fan-DAN-go): A dancing party for the working people.

flauta de pan (FLAU-tah de PAHN): A wind instrument of South American origin consisting of several pipes of different lengths, strapped together and played by blowing across the top.

guajira (gua-HEE-rah): A Cuban story song and dance.

guaracha (gua-RAH-cha): An Afro-Cuban song popular in the nineteenth century.

güiro (GEE-roh): A scraper made of a hollowed notched gourd with frets. It makes a loud, raspy sound.

guitar: A six-string instrument with a neck.

guitarrilla (gee-tah-RREE-ya): A small four-string guitar used to accompany folk songs and dances in Bolivia, Guatemala, and Peru.

guitarrón (gee-tah-RROHN): A large four-string bass guitar from Chile and Mexico.

huapango (hwa-PAHN-goh): A native dance from the Gulf Coast of northern Mexico.

mambo (MAHM-boh): A dance derived from the Cuban rumba.

maracas (mah-RAH-cas): Rattles made from gourds with dried seeds inside. They can also be made of wood or metal.

mariachis (mah-ree-AH-chees): A Mexican street band that plays traditional music.

marimba (mah-REEM-bah): An instrument similar to the African xylophone.

música norteña (MOO-zee-kah nor-TAYN-yah): Music of the U.S.-Mexican border. Includes conjunto music and orquesta tejana.

orquesta (or-KAYS-tah): A Mexican or Mexican American "orchestra," or band.

percussive instruments: Instruments that are played by striking them with a stick or by shaking them.

plena (PLAY-nah): A lively, funny story set to music, usually sung by Puerto Rican townspeople.

porro (POH-rroh): A Colombian dance.

posada (poh-SAH-dah): A Christmas song.

quebradita (kay-bray-DEE-tah): A dance that combines four other dances: two-step, salsa, flamenco, and tango.

quena (KAY-nah): An open-notched flute from Peru, made of bone, clay, gourd, or metal.

requinto (re-KEEN-toh): A small guitar with four courses of strings. Used in Colombia, Ecuador, and Mexico.

rumba (ROOM-bah): An Afro-Cuban music and dance popular in the 1930's.

salsa (SAHL-sah): A Latino dance music of Afro-Cuban origin.

samba (SAHM-bah): A Brazilian dance.

son (SOHN): A type of song using African rhythms and African instruments.

syncopation: Accented beats that break the regular pattern of the music.

tambora (tam-BOH-rah): A drum.

timbales (teem-BAH-les): Kettledrums made of metal shells.

tiple (TEE-play): An Colombian instrument like a guitar, with four courses of triple metal strings that are strummed but not plucked.

vals jota (vals-HOH-tah): A social dance popular in the nineteenth century. It was danced by the upper class.

vaquero (vah-KAY-roh): A cowboy song. Also, a cowboy.

zapateado (zah-pah-tay-AH-doh): A dance that uses strong foot stamping, called clogging.

MORE ABOUT LATINO MUSIC AND DANCE

Loza, Steven. *Barrio Rhythm: Mexican American Music in Los Angeles*. Urbana: University of Illinois Press, 1993.

Manuel, Peter. "Latin America and the Caribbean." In *Popular Musics of the Non-Western World*. New York: Oxford University Press, 1988.

Padilla, Felix M. "Salsa: Puerto Rican and Latin Music." *Journal of Popular Culture* 24, no. 1 (1990): 87-104.

Paredes, Américo. *A Texas-Mexican Cancionero: Folksongs of the Lower Border*. Durham, N.C.: Duke University Press, 1976.

_____. *The Texas-Mexican Conjunto: History of Working-Class Music*. Austin: University of Texas Press, 1985.

_____. *"With His Pistol in His Hand": A Border Ballad and Its Hero*. Austin: University of Texas Press, 1958.

Peña, Manuel. "Music." In *The Hispanic American Almanac*, edited by Nicolas Kanellos. Detroit: Gale Research, 1993.

_____. *The Texas-Mexican Conjunto*. Austin: University of Texas Press, 1985.

INDEX

African music and dance 14-16
Afro-Cubans 36
Aguinaldo 31
Alabados 18
Arizona 21-24
Arnaz, Desi 34
Autos sacramentales 13, 23

Bailes 19
Banda 21
Barretto, Ray 39
Batuque 16
Blades, Rubén 32, 40
Bomba 31
Boston, Tony 32

California 18-21
Canción 18
Castro, Fidel 33
Cha-cha-cha 36
Chicanos 7
Christmas 23
Cinco de Mayo 24, 27
Clave 31
Conga 16, 35
Conjunto music 26
Contradanza 19
Corridos 9, 24, 26
Cruz, Celia 40
Cuban American music and dance 7, 33-38
Cumbia 16

Décima 18
Devil dance 14
Día de los Muertos 23
Dieciséis de Septiembre 27

El Venado 14
Estefan, Gloria 41

Fandangos 20
Fender, Freddy 41
Fiesta de Nuestra Señora 23
Fiesta de Santa Fe 24
Flutes 13
Folk music and dance 9, 21

Gillespie, Dizzy 36

I Love Lucy 34
Incas 11
Indian civilizations 11

Jarabe Tapatío 14, 24
Jazz 36-38

Latin Empire 32
Latin hip-hop 38
Los Viejitos 24

Mambo 31, 36
Mariachis 18
Mariel boat lift 38
Mayas 11
Mendes, Sergio 41
Mestizos 7
Mexican American music and dance 7, 17-28
Miami, Florida 33-36
Missionaries and missions 13, 18
Moreno, Rita 41
Música norteña 26

Navidad 23
New Mexico 21-24
New Orleans, Louisiana 36-38
Northeast 7, 29-32
Nuyoricans 29

Orquesta music 21, 27
Percussive instruments 16
Piñata 24
Plena 31
Popular music 9
Porro 16
Posadas 18
Posadas, Las 23-24
Pozo, Chano 36
Puente, Tito 43
Puerto Rican music and dance 7, 29-32

Quebradita 21

Rap 32
Representaciones 23
Rhythm 9
Rivera, Chita 43
Rodriguez, Rick 32
Ronstadt, Linda 43
Rumba 16, 35

Salsa 9, 30-32, 37
Samba 16
Santana, Carlos 43
Son 31
Southeast 7, 33-38
Southwest 7, 17-28
Spanglish 32
Spaniards 13-14
Syncopation 35

Texas 24, 26-28

Valens, Ritchie 43
Vals jota 19
Vaqueros 18

Zapateado 21